TEXTS FOR STUDENTS. No. 5

GENERAL EDITORS· Caroline A. J. Skeel, D.Lit.;
H. J White, D.D.; J. P Whitney, B.D., D C.L.

A TRANSLATION OF THE

LATIN WRITINGS OF ST. PATRICK

BY

NEWPORT J. D. WHITE, D.D.

CANON OF ST PATRICK'S
AND ARCHBISHOP KING'S PROFESSOR IN THE UNIVERSITY OF DUBLIN

LONDON
SOCIETY FOR PROMOTING
CHRISTIAN KNOWLEDGE
1918

INTRODUCTION

St. Patrick's *Confession* and *Letter* are the two oldest writings connected with Christianity in Ireland. St. Patrick went there as missionary bishop in A.D. 432, and died in A.D. 461. The *Confession*, which is the Saint's self vindication, seems to have been composed towards the close of his career, perhaps about A.D. 450, and the *Letter* may be later than the *Confession*. The *Letter* is a manifesto called forth by a piratical raid on Ireland by a British Chieftain, Coroticus or Coriticus.

There can be no reasonable doubt as to the authenticity of these writings. They have a ring of unmistakable sincerity and genuineness, and contain strong internal evidence that they belong to the fifth century A.D.: (1) The text of the Latin Bible used by the author is, in the O.T., that current before St. Jerome published his retranslation from the Hebrew (A.D. 391-404); while the quotations from the N.T. seem to follow partly St. Jerome's revision (A.D. 383) and partly the earlier versions. The author's N.T., in fact, was of the type current in South Gaul, where there is reason to believe St. Patrick was educated. (2) The Franks are alluded to as heathens in *Letter*, c. 14; in A.D. 496 they followed their king, Clovis, into the Christian Church. (3) There are polemical allusions to sun-worship in *Confession*, cc. 20, 60. This was a prominent feature in the religion of Mithraism, which was popular all over the Roman Empire during the first four and five centuries of our era. Other points more or less favourable to the date claimed for these writings are: the style of Latin, the references to the Roman organization of Britain, the casual mention of a married clergy (*Confession*, c. 1), and the application of the term "apostate" to the Picts (*Letter*, cc. 2, 15). St. Ninian's mission to the Picts is dated A.D. 398-432 or earlier.

The Latin text underlying this translation is a revision of that published by the present writer in 1905 (*Proceedings, Royal Irish Academy*, xxv., C. 7). The manuscripts known to exist are seven in number; the oldest being that contained in the Book of Armagh, transcribed between A.D. 807 and 846. The other MSS. belong to the tenth, eleventh, and twelfth centuries. The Book of Armagh does not contain the *Letter*; and the copy of the *Confession* followed by the scribe was mutilated and in parts illegible. A critical account of these MSS. will be found in the edition mentioned above, and also in a paper on the Paris MS. published in *Proceedings, R.I.A.*, xxv., C., 11.

Apart from their value as an expression of religious experience, these two little books have a special historical significance. St. Patrick was a great Christian missionary, and, as such, an agent in the spread of Christian civilization. Ireland, unfortunately, never came under the moulding influences of the Roman Empire; and it was the mission of St. Patrick, consciously undertaken, to bring Irish Christianity into line with that of the Roman Empire, and thus undo the unfortunate consequences of the Cæsars' negligence or impotence. St. Patrick, a British Celt, was proud of his citizenship in the empire of Rome, which, even in its decadence, was to him conterminous with Christian civilization.

ST. PATRICK'S CONFESSION AND LETTER

THE CONFESSION

[*As far as possible, in the quotations from the Bible, which are printed in italics, the rendering of the English Version of* 1611 *has been followed, except in O-T. Apocrypha, in which the Douay Version of* 1609 *has been used.*]

1. I, Patrick the sinner, am the most clownish and the least of all the faithful, and contemptible in the eyes of very many.

My father was Calpornus, a deacon, one of the sons of Potitus, a presbyter, who belonged to the village of Banavem Taberniæ. Now he had a small farm hard by, where I was taken captive.

I was then about sixteen years of age. I knew not the true God; and I went into captivity to Ireland with many thousands of persons, according to our deserts, because we departed away from God, and kept not his commandments, and were not obedient to our priests, who used to admonish us for our salvation. And the Lord *poured upon us the fury of his anger,* and scattered us amongst many heathen, even *unto the ends of the earth,* where now my littleness may be seen amongst men of another nation.

2. And there the Lord *opened the understanding* of my unbelief that, even though late, I might call my faults to

---

1. Is. xlii. 25 ; Acts xiii. 47.
2. Luke xxiv. 45.

remembrance, and that I might *turn with all my heart* to the Lord my God, who *regarded* my *low estate,* and pitied the youth of my ignorance, and kept me before I knew him, and before I had discernment or could distinguish between good and evil, and protected me and comforted me as a father does his son.

3. Wherefore then I cannot keep silence—nor would it be fitting—concerning such great benefits and such great grace as the Lord hath vouchsafed to bestow on me in the land of my captivity; because this is what we can render unto him, namely, that after we have been chastened, and have come to the knowledge of God, we shall exalt and *praise his wondrous works* before *every nation which is under the whole heaven.*

4. Because there is no other God, nor was there ever any in times past, nor shall there be hereafter, except God the Father unbegotten, without beginning, from whom all things take their beginning, holding all things [*i.e.,* Almighty], as we say, and his Son Jesus Christ, whom we affirm verily to have always existed with the Father before the creation of the world, with the Father after the manner of a spiritual existence, begotten ineffably, before the beginning of anything. And *by him* were made *things visible and invisible.* He was made man ; and, having overcome death, he was received up into heaven to the Father And *he gave to him all power above every name of things in heaven and things in earth and things under the earth ; and let every tongue confess to him that Jesus Christ is Lord and God* in whom we believe. And we look for his coming soon to be; he the Judge of the quick and the dead, *who will render to every man according to his deeds.* And *he shed on*

2 Joel ii. 12 ; Luke i. 48.
3. Ps. lxxxix. 5 ; Acts ii 5
4, Col i. 16 ; Phil. ii, 9-11 ; Rom. ii. 6 ; Tit. iii, 5, 6,

us abundantly the Holy Ghost, the gift and earnest of immortality, who makes those who believe and obey to become *children of God* the Father and *joint heirs with Christ,* whom we confess and adore as one God in the Trinity of the Holy Name.

5. For he himself hath said through the prophet, *Call upon me in the day of trouble ; I will deliver thee, and thou shalt glorify me.* And again he saith, *It is honourable to reveal and confess the works of God.*

6. Nevertheless, although I am faulty in many things, I wish my brethren and kinsfolk to know what manner of man I am, and that they may be able to understand the desire of my soul.

7. I am not ignorant of *the testimony of my Lord,* who witnesseth in the Psalm, *Thou shalt destroy them that speak a lie.* And again he saith, *The mouth that belieth killeth the soul.* And the same Lord saith in the Gospel, *The idle word that men shall speak, they shall give account thereof in the day of judgement.*

8. Wherefore then I ought exceedingly, *with fear and trembling,* to dread this sentence in that day when no one will be able to absent himself or hide, but when all of us, without exception, shall have *to give account* of even the smallest sins *before the judgement seat of* the Lord *Christ.*

9. On this account I had long since thought of writing ; but I hesitated until now ; for I feared lest I should fall under the censure of men's tongues, and because I have not studied as have others, who in the most approved fashion have drunk in both law and the Holy Scriptures alike, and have never changed their speech from their infancy, but rather have been always rendering it more perfect.

4. Rom. viii. 16, 17.
5. Ps. l. 15 ; Tob. xii. 7.
7. 2 Tim. i. 8 ; Ps. v. 6 ; Wisd. i. 11 ; Matt. xii. 36.
8. Eph. vi. 5 ; Rom. xiv. 10, 12.

For my speech and language is translated into a tongue
not my own, as can be easily proved from the savour of my
writing, in what fashion I have been taught and am learned
in speech; for, saith the wise man, *By the tongue will be dis-*
covered understanding and knowledge and the teaching of truth.

10. But what avails an excuse, no matter how true,
especially when accompanied by presumption ? since now
I myself, in mine old age, earnestly desire that which in
youth I did not acquire; because my sins prevented me
from mastering what I had read through before. But
who gives me credence even if I should repeat the state-
ment that I made at the outset?

When a youth, nay, almost a boy, I went into captivity
in language [as well as in person] before I knew what I
should earnestly desire, or what I ought to shun. And so
to-day I blush and am exceedingly afraid to lay bare my
lack of education; because I am unable to make my mean-
ing plain in a few words to the learned , for as the Spirit
yearns, the [human] disposition displays the souls of men
and their understandings.

11. But if I had had [only] the same privileges as others,
nevertheless I would not keep silence *on account of the*
reward. And if perchance it seems to not a few that I am
thrusting myself forward in this matter with my want of
knowledge and my *slow tongue,* yet it is written, *The tongue*
of the stammerers shall quickly learn to speak peace. How
much rather should we earnestly desire so to do, who are,
he saith, *the epistle of Christ for salvation unto the ends of the*
earth, although not a learned one, yet *ministered* most
powerfully, *written in your hearts, not with ink, but with the*
Spirit of the living God. And again the Spirit witnesseth,
And husbandry [lit. *rusticity*] *was ordained by the Most High.*

---

9 Ecclus iv. 29
11. Ps. cxix 112 ; Exod. iv. 10 ; Is. xxxii. 4 ; 2 Cor. iii. 2, 3 ,
Acts xiii. 47 ; Ecclus. vii. 16.

12. Whence I who was at first a clown, an exile, unlearned verily, who know not how to provide for the future—but this I do know most surely, that *before I was afflicted* I was like a stone lying in the deep mire; and *he that is mighty* came, and in his mercy lifted me up, and verily raised me aloft and placed me on the top of the wall. And therefore I ought to cry aloud that I may also *render somewhat to the Lord* for his benefits which are so great both here and in eternity, the value of which the mind of men cannot estimate.

13. Wherefore then be ye astonied, *ye that fear God, both small and great,* and ye clever sirs, ye rhetoricians, hear therefore and search it out. Who was it that called up me, fool though I be, out of the midst of those who seem to be wise and skilled in the law, and *powerful in word and in everything?* And me, moreover, the abhorred of this world, did he inspire beyond others—if such I were —only that *with reverence and godly fear* and *unblameably* I should faithfully be of service to the nation to whom the love of Christ conveyed me, and presented me, as long as I live, if I should be worthy; in fine, that I should with humility and in truth diligently do them service.

14. And so it is proper that according to *the proportion of faith* in the Trinity, I should define doctrine, and make known the gift of God and *everlasting consolation, without being held back* by danger, and spread everywhere the name of God without fear, confidently; so that even *after my decease* I may leave a legacy to my brethren and sons whom I baptized in the Lord, many thousands of persons.

15. And I was not worthy, nor such an one, as that the

---

12. Ps. cxix. 67 ; Luke i 49 ; Ps. cxvi. 12.
13. Rev. xix. 5 ; Acts vii. 22 ; Heb. xii 28 , 1 Thess. ii 10.
14. Rom. xii 3; 2 Thess ii 16 ; Phil ii. 15 ; 2 Pet. i. 15.

Lord should grant this to his poor servant, after calamities and such great difficulties, after a life of slavery, after many years; that he should bestow on me so great grace towards that nation, a thing that formerly, in my youth, I never hoped for nor thought of.

16. Now, after I came to Ireland, tending flocks was my daily occupation; and constantly I used to pray in the day time. Love of God and the fear of him increased more and more, and faith grew, and the spirit was moved, so that in one day [I would say] as many as a hundred prayers, and at night nearly as many, so that I used to stay even in the woods and on the mountain [to this end]. And before daybreak I used to be roused to prayer, in snow, in frost, in rain; and I felt no hurt; nor was there any sluggishness in me—as I now see, because then *the spirit was fervent* within me.

17. And there verily one night I heard in my sleep a voice saying to me, "Thou fastest to good purpose, thou who art soon to go to thy fatherland." And again, after a very short time, I heard the answer [of God] saying to me, "Lo, thy ship is ready." And it was not near at hand, but was perhaps distant two hundred miles. And I had never been there, nor did I know anyone there. And thereupon I shortly took to flight, and left the man with whom I had been for six years, and I came in the strength of God who prospered my way for good, and I met with nothing to alarm me until I reached that ship.

18. And on the very day that I arrived, the ship left its moorings, and I said that I had to [*or* must] sail thence with them; but the shipmaster was annoyed, and replied

16. Acts xviii. 25.

roughly and angrily, "On no account seek to go with us."

When I heard this, I parted from them to go to the hut where I was lodging, and on the way I began to pray, and before I had finished my prayer, I heard one of them shouting loudly after me, "Come quickly, for these men are calling thee;" and straightway I returned to them.

And they began to say to me, "Come, for we receive thee in good faith; make friends with us in any way thou desirest." And so on that day I refused to be intimate with them [*lit.* suck their breasts], because of the fear of God; but nevertheless I hoped that some of them would come into the faith of Jesus Christ, for they were heathen; and on this account I continued with them; and forthwith we set sail.

19. And after three days we reached land, and journeyed for twenty-eight days through a desert; and food failed them, and hunger overcame them. And one day the shipmaster began to say to me, "How is this, O Christian? thou sayest that thy God is great and almighty; wherefore then canst thou not pray for us, for we are in danger of starvation? Hardly shall we ever see a human being again."

Then said I plainly to them, "*Turn* in good faith and *with all your heart to* the Lord my God, to whom nothing is impossible, that this day he may send you food in your journey until ye be satisfied, for he has abundance everywhere."

And, by the help of God, so it came to pass. Lo, a herd of swine appeared in the way before our eyes, and they killed many of them; and in that place they remained two nights, and they were well refreshed, and their dogs

19 Joel ii. 12.

were sated, for many of them had fainted and were *left half dead* by the way.

And after this they rendered hearty thanks to God, and I became honourable in their eyes; and from that day on they had food in abundance. Moreover, they found wild honey, and *gave* me *a piece of it.* And one of them said, "*This is offered in sacrifice.*" Thanks be to God, I tasted none of it.

20. Now on that same night, when I was sleeping, Satan tempted me mightily, in such sort as I shall remember *as long as I am in this body.* And there fell upon me as it were a huge rock, and I had no power over my limbs. But whence did it occur to me—to my ignorant mind—to call upon Helias? And on this I saw the sun rise in the heaven, and while I was shouting "Helias" with all my might, lo, the splendour of that sun fell upon me, and straightway shook all weight from off me. And I believe that I was helped by Christ my Lord, and that his Spirit was even then calling aloud on my behalf, And I trust that it will be so *in the day of* my *trouble,* as he saith in the Gospel, *In that day,* the Lord testifieth, *it is not ye that speak, but the Spirit of your Father which speaketh in you.*

21. And, again, after many years, I went into captivity once more. And so on that first night I remained with them. Now I heard the answer of God saying to me, "For two months thou shalt be with them." And so it came to pass. On the sixtieth night after, the Lord delivered me out of their hands.

22. Moreover, he provided for us on our journey food and fire and dry quarters every day, until on the fourteenth day we reached human habitations. As I stated above,

19. Luke x. 30; xxiv. 12; 1 Cor. x. 28.
20. 2 Pet. i. 13; Ps. l. 15; Matt. x. 20.

for twenty-eight days we journeyed through a desert; and on the night on which we reached human habitations, we had in truth no food left.

23. And again, after a few years, I was in Britain with my kindred, who received me as a son, and in good faith besought me that at all events now, after the great tribulations which I had undergone, I would not depart from them anywhither.

And there verily *I saw in the night visions* a man whose name was Victoricus coming as it were from Ireland with countless letters. And he gave me one of them, and I read the beginning of the letter, which was entitled, "The Voice of the Irish"; and while I was reading aloud the beginning of the letter, I thought that at that very moment I heard the voice of them who lived beside the wood of Foclut[1] which is nigh unto the western sea: And thus they cried, as with one mouth, "We beseech thee, holy youth, to come and walk among us once more."

And I was exceedingly *broken in heart*, and could read no further. And so I awoke. Thanks be to God that after very many years the Lord granted to them according to their cry.

24. And another night, whether within me or beside me, *I cannot tell, God knoweth*, in most admirable words which I heard and could not understand, except that at the end of the prayer he thus affirmed, "He who *laid down his life for thee*, he it is who speaketh in thee." And so I awoke, rejoicing.

25. And another time I saw him praying within me, and I was as it were within my body; and I heard [One

23. Dan vii. 13; Ps. cix. 16   24. 2 Cor. xii. 2; John x. 11.
25. Eph iii. 16.

[1] In Co. Mayo.

praying] over me, that is, over *the inner man*, and there he was praying mightily with groanings. And meanwhile I was astonied, and was marvelling and thinking who it could be that was praying within me; but at the end of the prayer he affirmed that he was the Spirit. And so I awoke, and I remembered how the apostle saith, *The Spirit helpeth the infirmities of our prayer, for we know not what we should pray for as we ought; but the Spirit himself maketh intercession for us with groanings which cannot be uttered, which cannot be expressed in words.* And again, *The Lord our Advocate maketh intercession for us.*

26. And when I was tempted by not a few of my elders, who came and [urged] my sins against my laborious episcopate—certainly on that day *I was sore thrust at that I might fall* both here and in eternity. But the Lord graciously spared the stranger and sojourner for his name's sake; and he helped me exceedingly when I was thus trampled on, so that I did not come badly into disgrace and reproach. I pray God *that it may not be laid to their charge* as sin.

27. After the lapse of thirty years *they found,* as an *occasion* against me, a matter which I had confessed before I was a deacon. Because of anxiety, with sorrowful mind, I disclosed to my dearest friend things that I had done in my youth one day, nay, in one hour, because I had not yet overcome. *I cannot tell, God knoweth,* if I was then fifteen years old; and I did not believe in the living God, nor had I since my infancy; but I remained in death and in unbelief until I had been chastened exceedingly, and humbled in truth by hunger and nakedness, and that daily.

28. Contrariwise, I did not proceed to Ireland of my own accord until I was nearly worn out. But this was

25 Rom. viii. 26; 1 John ii. 1; Rom. viii. 34.
26. Ps. cxviii. 13; 2 Tim. iv. 16.   27. Dan. vi 5; 2 Cor. xii. 2.

rather well for me, because thus I was amended by the
Lord. And he fitted me, so that I should to-day be some-
thing which was once far from me, that I should care for,
or be busy about, the salvation of others, whereas then I
did not even think about myself.

29. And so on that day on which I was disapproved of
by the aforesaid persons whom I have mentioned, in that
night *I saw in the night visions:*—There was a writing void
of honour against my face. And meanwhile I heard the
answer of God saying to me, "We have seen with anger
the face of the person designated (the name being expressed)." Nor did he say thus, "Thou hast seen with
anger," but, "We have seen with anger," as if in that
matter he had joined himself [with me]. As he said, *He
that toucheth you is as he that toucheth the apple of mine eye.*

30. Therefore *I thank him who hath enabled me* in all
things, because he did not hinder me from the journey on
which I had resolved, and from my labour which I had
learnt from Christ my Lord, but rather *I felt in myself* no
little *virtue proceeding from him,* and my *faith has been
approved in the sight of God and of men.*

31. Wherefore then *I say boldly* that my conscience does
not blame me either here or hereafter. God is my witness
that I have not lied in the matters that I have stated
to you.

32. But rather I am grieved for my dearest friend that
we should have deserved to hear such an answer as that;
a man to whom I had even entrusted my soul! And I
ascertained from not a few of the brethren before that
contention—it was at a time when I was not present, nor
was I in Britain, nor will the story originate with me—
that he too had fought for me in my absence. Even he

29. Dan. vii. 13; Zech. ii. 8
30. 1 Tim. i. 12; Mark v. 29, 30; 1 Pet. i. 7; 2 Cor. viii. 21.
31. Acts ii. 29.

himself had said to me with his own lips, "Lo, thou art to be raised to the rank of bishop;" of which I was not worthy. But how did it occur to him afterwards to put me to shame publicly before everyone, good and bad, in respect of an [office] which before that he had of his own accord and gladly conceded [to me], and the Lord too, who is *greater than all ?*

33. I have said enough. Nevertheless I ought not to hide the gift of God which he bestowed upon us in the land of my captivity; because then I earnestly sought him, and there I found him, and he kept me from all iniquities—this is my belief—*because of his indwelling Spirit* who hath worked in me until this day. Boldly again [am I speaking]. But God knoweth if man had said this to me—perchance I would have held my peace for the love of Christ.

34. Hence therefore I render unwearied thanks to my God who kept me faithful *in the day of* my *temptation,* so that to-day I can confidently offer to him a sacrifice, as *a living victim,* my soul to Christ my Lord who *saved me out of all my troubles,* so that I may say, *Who am I, O Lord,* or what is my calling, that thou hast worked together with me with such divine power? so that to day among the heathen I should steadfastly exult, and magnify thy name wherever I may be; and that not only in prosperity, but also in troubles, so that whatever may happen to me, whether good or bad, I ought to receive it with an equal mind, and ever render thanks to God who shewed me that I might trust him endlessly, as one that cannot be doubted; and who heard me, so that I, ignorant as I am, and *in the last days,* should be bold to undertake this work so holy and so wonderful; so that I might imitate, in some degree,

32. John x. 29.   33. Rom viii. 11.
34. Ps. xcv. 8; Rom xii. 1; Ps. xxxiv. 6; 2 Sam. vii. 18; Acts ii. 17.

those of whom the Lord long ago foretold when foreshow-
ng that his *Gospel would be for a witness unto all nations*
before *the end* of the world.   And accordingly, as we see,
this has been so fulfilled.   Behold, we are witnesses that
the Gospel has been preached to the limit beyond which
no man dwells.

35. Now it were a tedious task to *declare particularly* the
whole of my toil, or even partially [*or*, and in all its
parts].   I shall briefly say in what manner the most
righteous God often delivered me from slavery and from
twelve perils whereby my soul was endangered, besides
many plots and *things which I am not able to express in words.*
Nor shall I weary my readers.   But I have as my voucher
God who knoweth all things even before they come to
pass, as the answer of God frequently warned me, the poor,
unlearned orphan.

36. Whence came to me this wisdom, which was not in
me, I who neither *knew the number of my days,* nor cared
for God?   Whence afterwards came to me that gift so
great, so salutary, the knowledge and love of God, but only
that I might part with fatherland and kindred?

37. And many gifts were proffered me with weeping and
tears.   And I displeased them, and also, against my wish,
not a few of my elders ; but, God being my guide, in no
way did I consent or yield to them.   It was not any grace
in me, but God who overcometh in me ; and he withstood
them all, so that I came to the heathen Irish to preach the
Gospel, and to endure insults from unbelievers, so as to
hear the reproach of my going abroad, and [endure] many
persecutions *even unto bonds,* and that I should give up my
free condition for the profit of others.   And if I should be
worthy, I am ready [to give] even my life *for his name's*

---

34. Matt. xxiv. 14.   35. Acts xxi. 19 , Rom. viii. 26.
36 Ps xxxix. 4   37. Ecclus. xxix. 29 ; 2 Tim. ii. 9.

sake unhesitatingly and very gladly; and there I desire to spend it even unto death, if the Lord would grant it to me.

38. Because I am a debtor exceedingly to God, who granted me such great grace that many peoples through me should be regenerated to God and afterwards confirmed, and that clergy should everywhere be ordained for them, for a people newly come to belief, which the Lord took *from the ends of the earth*, as he had in times past promised through his prophets: *The Gentiles shall come unto thee from the ends of the earth, and shall say, As our fathers have got for themselves false idols and there is no profit in them.* And again, *I have set thee to be a light of the Gentiles, that thou shouldest be for salvation unto the ends of the earth.*

39. And there I wish to *wait for his promise* who verily never disappoints. As he promises in the Gospel, *They shall come from the east and west and from the south and from the north, and shall sit down with Abraham and Isaac and Jacob;* as we believe that believers will come from all parts of the world.

40. For that reason therefore, we ought to fish well and diligently, as the Lord forewarns and teaches, saying, *Come ye after me, and I will make you to become fishers of men.* And again, he saith through the prophets, *Behold I send fishers and many hunters, saith God,* and so forth.

Wherefore then, it was exceedingly necessary that we should spread our nets so that a *great multitude* and a throng should be taken for God, and that everywhere there should be clergy to baptize and exhort a people poor and needy, as the Lord in the Gospel warns and teaches, saying, *Go ye therefore now and teach all nations, baptizing them in the name of the Father, and of the Son, and of the Holy*

37. 3 John 7.
38. Jer. xvi. 19; Acts xiii. 47.   39. Acts i. 4; Matt. viii. 11
40. Matt. iv. 19; Jer. xvi. 16, Luke v. 6; Matt. xxviii. 19.

Ghost: teaching them to observe all things whatsoever I have commanded you: and, lo, I am with you alway, even unto the end of the world. And again he saith, *Go ye therefore into all the world, and preach the Gospel to every creature. He that believeth and is baptized shall be saved; but he that believeth not shall be damned.* And again, *This Gospel of the kingdom shall be preached in all the world for a witness unto all nations, and then shall the end come.*

And in like manner the Lord, foreshowing by the prophet, saith, *And it shall come to pass in the last days, saith the Lord, I will pour out of my Spirit upon all flesh: and your sons and your daughters shall prophesy, and your young men shall see visions, and your old men shall dream dreams: and on my servants and on my handmaidens I will pour out in those days of my Spirit; and they shall prophesy.* And Osee saith, *I will call them my people, which were not my people; and her one that hath obtained mercy which had not obtained mercy. And it shall come to pass, that in the place where it was said, Ye are not my people; there shall they be called the children of the living God.*

41. Wherefore then in Ireland they who never had the knowledge of God, but until now only worshipped idols and abominations—how has there been lately *prepared a people* of the Lord, and they are called children of God? Sons and daughters of Scottic chieftains are seen to become monks and virgins of Christ.

42. In especial there was one blessed lady of Scottic birth, of noble rank, most beautiful, grown up, whom I baptized; and after a few days she came to us for a certain cause. She disclosed to us that she had been warned by an angel of God, and that he counselled her to become a virgin of Christ, and live closer to God. Thanks be to

40. Mark xvi. 15; Matt. xxiv. 14; Acts ii. 17, 18; Rom. ix. 25, 26. **41.** Luke i. 17.

God, six days after, most admirably and eagerly she seized on that which all virgins of God do in like manner ; not with the consent of their fathers ; but they endure persecution and lying reproaches from their kindred ; and nevertheless their number increases more and more—and as for those of our race who are born there, we know not the number of them—besides widows and continent persons.

But the women who are kept in slavery suffer especially ; they constantly endure even unto terrors and threats. But the Lord gave grace to many of his handmaidens, for although they are forbidden, they earnestly follow the example [set them].

43. Wherefore then, even if I should wish to part with them, and thus proceeding to Britain—and glad and ready I was to do so—as to my fatherland and kindred, and not that only, but to go as far as Gaul in order to visit the brethren and to behold the face of the saints of my Lord— God knoweth that I used to desire it exceedingly—yet *I am bound in the Spirit,* who *witnesseth to me* that if I should do ·this, he would note me as guilty ; and I fear to lose the labour which I began, and yet not I, but Christ the Lord who commanded me to come and be with them for the remainder of my life, if the Lord will, and if he should keep me from every evil way, so that I may not sin in his sight.

44. Now I hope that I ought to do this ; but I do not trust myself *as long as I am in the body of this death,* because he is strong who daily endeavours to turn me away from the faith, and from that chastity of unfeigned religion which I have purposed to keep to the end of my life for Christ my Lord. But the flesh, the enemy, is ever dragging us unto death, that is, to enticements to do that

---

43. Acts xx. 22, 23.
44 2 Pet. i. 13 ; Rom. vii. 24.

which is forbidden. And *I know in part* wherein I have not led a perfect life as have other believers; but I confess to my Lord, and I do not blush in his presence, for I lie not. From the time that I knew him, from my youth, there grew in me the love of God and the fear of him; and unto this hour, the Lord being gracious to me, *I have kept the faith.*

45. Let who will laugh and insult, I shall not be silent nor conceal the signs and wonders which were shewn to me by the Lord many years before they came to pass; since he knoweth all things even *before the world began.*

46. Wherefore then I ought without ceasing to render thanks to God who oftentimes pardoned my folly and carelessness—and that not in one place only—so that he be not exceedingly wroth with me, to whom I have been given as a fellow-labourer; and yet I did not quickly yield in accordance with what had been shewn to me, and as *the Spirit brought to my remembrance.* And the Lord *shewed mercy upon me thousands of times,* because he saw in me that I was ready, but that I did not know through these [revelations] what I should do about my position, because many were forbidding this embassage. Moreover they used to talk amongst themselves behind my back and say, "Why does this fellow thrust himself into danger amongst hostile people *who know not God?*" They did not say this out of malice; but it did not seem meet in their eyes, on account of my clownishness, as I myself witness that I have understood. And I did not quickly recognize the grace that was then in me. Now that seems meet in mine eyes which I ought to have done before.

47. Now therefore, I have frankly disclosed to my brethren and fellow-servants who have believed me, for what reason *I told you before, and foretell you* to strengthen

---

44. 1 Cor. xiii. 9; 2 Tim. iv. 7   45. 2 Tim. i. 9.
46. John xiv. 26; Exod. xx. 6; 2 Thess. i. 8.   47. 2 Cor. xiii. 2.

and confirm your faith. Would that you, too, would imitate greater things, and do things of more consequence. This will be my glory, for *a wise son is the glory of his father.*

48. You know, and God also, in what manner I have lived from my youth with you, in the faith of truth and in sincerity of heart. Moreover as regards those heathen amongst whom I dwell, I have kept faith with them, and will keep it. God knoweth I have *defrauded none* of them, nor do I think of doing it, for the sake of God and his Church, lest I should raise persecution against them and all of us, and lest through me the name of the Lord should be blasphemed, for it is written, *Woe to the man through whom the name of the Lord is blasphemed.*

49. *But though I be rude in all things,* nevertheless I have endeavoured in some sort to keep myself, both for the Christian brethren, and the virgins of Christ, and the *devout women* who used of their own accord to present me with their little gifts, and would cast of their ornaments upon the altar; and I returned them again to them. And they were scandalized at my doing so. But I did it on account of the hope of immortality, so as to keep myself warily in all things; for this reason, namely, that the heathen might receive me and the ministry of my service on any grounds, and that I should not, even in the smallest matter, give occasion to the unbelievers to defame or disparage.

50. Perchance then, when I baptized so many thousands of men, I hoped from any one of them even as much as the half of a scruple. *Tell me and I shall restore it to you.* Or when the Lord ordained clergy everywhere by means of my mediocrity, and I imparted my service to them for nothing, if I demanded from one of them even the price of my *shoe; tell it against me and I shall restore you* more.

---

47. Prov. x. 1.   48 2 Cor. vii. 2; Matt xviii. 7; Rom. ii. 24.
49. 2 Cor. xi. 6; Acts xiii. 50.   50. 1 Sam. xii. 3.

51. *I spent for you* that they might receive me ; and both amongst you and wherever I journeyed for your sake, through many perils, even to outlying regions beyond which no man dwelt, and where never had anyone come to baptize, or ordain clergy, or confirm the people, I have, by the bounty of the Lord, initiated everything, carefully and very gladly, for your salvation.

52. On occasion, I used to give presents to the kings, besides the hire that I gave to their sons who accompany me; and nevertheless they seized me with my companions. And on that day they most eagerly desired to kill me, but my time had not yet come. And everything they found with us they plundered, and me myself they bound with irons. And on the fourteenth day the Lord delivered me from their power, and whatever was ours was restored to us for the sake of God and the *near friends* whom we had provided beforehand.

53. Moreover, ye know by proof how much I paid to those who were judges throughout all the districts which I more frequently visited ; for I reckon that I distributed to them not less than the price of fifteen men, so that ye might enjoy me, and I might ever enjoy you in God. I do not regret it, nor is it enough for me. Still I *spend and will spend more.* The Lord is mighty to grant to me afterwards to be myself *spent for your souls.*

54. Behold, *I call God for a record upon my soul that I lie not ;* nor would I write to you that there may be *an occasion for flattering words or covetousness,* nor that I hope for honour from any of you. Sufficient to me is the honour which is not seen as yet, but is believed on in the heart. And *faithful is he that promised ;* never does he lie.

---

51. 2 Cor. xii. 15.
52. Acts x. 24.
53. 2 Cor. xii. 15.
54. 2 Cor. i. 23 ; Gal. i. 20 ; 1 Thess. ii. 5 , Heb x. 23.

55. But I see that already *in this present world* I am exalted above measure by the Lord. And I was not worthy nor such an one as that he should grant this to me; since I know most surely that poverty and affliction become me better than delights and riches. But Christ the Lord, too, was poor for our sakes; I indeed am wretched and unfortunate, and though I should wish for wealth, now I have it not, *nor do I judge mine own self;* for daily I expect either slaughter, or to be defrauded, or reduced to slavery, or an unfair attack of some kind. *But none of these things move me*, on account of the promises of heaven, because I have cast myself into the hands of God Almighty, for he rules everywhere, as saith the prophet, *Cast thy care upon God, and he shall sustain thee.*

56. Behold now *I commit the keeping of my soul to my most faithful* God, *for whom I am an ambassador* in my ignoble state, only because he accepteth no man's person and chose me for this duty that I should be one of his least ministers.

57. Wherefore then, *I shall render unto him for all his benefits* towards me. But what shall I say, or what shall I promise to my Lord? For I am only worth what he himself has given to me. But *he trieth the hearts and reins*, [and knoweth] that enough, and more than enough, do I desire, and was ready, that he should grant me to *drink of his cup*, as he granted to others also who love him.

58. On which account let it not happen to me from my God that I should ever part with his *people which he purchased* in the ends of the earth. I pray God to give me perseverance, and to vouchsafe that I bear to him faithful witness, until my passing hence, for the sake of my God.

---

55. Gal. i. 4 ; 1 Cor. iv. 3 ; Acts xx. 24 ; Ps. lv. 22.
56. 1 Pet. iv 19 ; Eph. vi. 20
57. Ps cxvi. 12 ; Ps. vii. 9 ; Matt. xx. 22.
58. Is. xliii. 21.

59. And if I ever imitated anything good for the sake of my God whom I love, I pray him to grant to me that I may shed my blood with those strangers and captives for his name's sake, even though I should lack burial itself, or that in most wretched fashion my corpse be divided limb by limb to dogs and wild beasts, or that the fowls of the air eat it. Most surely I deem that if this should happen to me, I have gained my soul as well as my body, because without any doubt we shall rise on that day in the clear shining of the sun, that is, in the glory of Christ Jesus our Redeemer, as *sons of the living God* and *joint heirs with Christ*, and *conformed to his image* that will be, since *of him and through him and in him* we shall reign.

60. For that sun which we behold, by the command of God rises daily for our sakes; but it will never reign, nor will its splendour endure; but all those who worship it shall—wretched men—come badly to punishment. We, on the other hand, who believe in and worship the true sun, Christ—who will never perish, nor will anyone *who doeth his will;* but he *will abide for ever,* as Christ *will abide for ever,* who reigneth with God the Father Almighty and with the Holy Spirit, before the worlds, and now, and for ever and ever. Amen.

61. Lo, again and again I shall briefly set forth the words of my confession: *I testify* in truth and in exultation of heart *before God and his holy angels,* that I never had any cause except the Gospel and his promises for ever returning to that nation from whence previously I scarcely escaped.

62. But I pray those who believe in and fear God, whosoever shall have vouchsafed to look upon and receive this

---

59. Rom. ix. 26 ; Rom. viii. 17, 29 ; Rom. xi. 36.
60. 1 John ii. 17 ; Ps. lxxxix. 36.
61. 1 Tim. v. 21.

writing which Patrick the sinner, unlearned verily, composed in Ireland, that no one ever say it was my ignorance
that did˙ whatever trifling matter I did, or proved, in
accordance with God's good pleasure ; but judge ye, and
let it be most truly believed that it was the gift of God.
And this is my confession before I die.

THE LETTER

1. Patrick the sinner, unlearned verily :—I confess that
I am a bishop, appointed by God, in Ireland. Most surely
I deem that from God I have received what I am. And so
I dwell in the midst of barbarians, a stranger and an exile
for the love of God. He is witness if this is so. Not that
I desired to utter from my mouth anything so harshly and
so roughly ; but I am compelled *by zeal for God ;* and *the
truth of Christ* roused me, for the love of my nearest friends
and sons, for whom I have *not regarded* my fatherland and
kindred, yea nor my *life even unto death,* if I am worthy. I
have vowed to my God to teach the heathen, though I be
despised by some.

2. With mine own hand have I written and composed
these words to be given and delivered and sent to the
soldiers of Coroticus—I do not say to my fellow-citizens or
to the fellow-citizens of the holy Romans, but to those who
are fellow-citizens of demons because of their evil deeds.
Behaving like enemies, they are dead while they live, allies
of the Scots and apostate Picts, as though wishing to gorge
themselves with blood, the blood of innocent Christians,
whom I in countless numbers begot to God and confirmed
in Christ.

1. Rom. x. 2; 2 Cor. xi. 10 ; Phil. ii. 30.

3. On the day following that on which the newly
baptized, in white array, were anointed—it was still
fragrant on their foreheads, while they were cruelly
butchered and slaughtered with the sword by the aforesaid
persons—I sent a letter with a holy presbyter whom I had
taught from his infancy, clergy accompanying him, with a
request that they would grant us some of the booty and
of the baptized captives whom they had taken. They
jeered at them.

4. Therefore I know not what I should the rather
mourn, whether those who are slain, or those whom they
captured, or those whom the devil grievously ensnared.
In everlasting punishment they will become slaves of hell
along with him, for verily *whosoever committeth sin is a
bondservant of sin*, and is called *a son of the devil*.

5. On this account let every man that feareth God learn
that aliens they are from me and from Christ my God, *for
whom I am an ambassador*—patricide, fratricide as he is!—
ravening wolves eating up the people of the Lord *as it were
bread*. As he saith, *O Lord, the ungodly have destroyed thy
law*, which in the last times he had excellently [and] kindly
planted in Ireland; and it was builded by the favour of
God.

6. I make no false claim. I have part with those whom
he called and predestinated to preach the Gospel amidst no
small persecutions, *even unto the ends of the earth*, even
though the enemy casts an evil eye on me by means of the
tyranny of Coroticus, who fears neither God nor his priests
whom he chose, and to whom he granted that highest,
divine, sublime power, that *whom they should bind on earth
should be bound in heaven*.

---

4. John viii. 34 ; Acts xiii. 10.
5. Eph. vi. 20 ; Acts xx. 29 ; Ps. xiv. 4 ; Ps. cxix. 126,
6. Rom. viii. 30 ; Acts xiii 47 ; Matt. xvi. 19,

7. Whence therefore, *ye holy and humble men of heart,* I beseech you very much. It is not right to pay court to such men, nor to take food or drink with them; nor ought one to accept their almsgivings, until [doing] sore penance with shedding of tears, they make amends to God, and liberate the servants of God and the baptized handmaidens of Christ, for whom he died and was crucified.

8. *The Most High approveth not the gifts of the wicked. He that offereth sacrifice of the goods of the poor is as one that sacrificeth the son in the presence of his father. The riches,* he saith, *which he hath gathered unjustly will be vomited up from his belly. The angel of death draggeth him away. He will be tormented by the fury of dragons. The viper's tongue shall slay him; unquenchable fire devoureth him.*

And therefore, *Woe to those who fill themselves with what is not their own.* And, *What is a man profited, if he shall gain the whole world, and lose his own soul?*

9. It would be tedious to discuss or declare [their deeds] one by one, [and] to gather from the whole law testimonies concerning such greed. Avarice is a deadly sin; *Thou shalt not covet thy neighbour's goods; Thou shalt do no murder; A murderer cannot be with Christ; He that hateth his brother is reckoned as a murderer.* And again, *He that loveth not his brother abideth in death.* How much more guilty is he that hath stained his hands with the blood of the sons of God whom he recently purchased in the ends of the earth through the exhortation of our littleness.

10. Was it without God, or according to the flesh, that I came to Ireland? Who compelled me? *I am bound in the Spirit* not to see any one of my kinsfolk. Is it from me that springs that godly compassion which I exercise

---

7. Dan. iii. 87.
8. Ecclus. xxxiv. 23, 24; Job xx. 15; Hab. ii. 6; Matt. xvi. 26.
9. Rom. xiii. 9; 1 John iii. 14, 15.
10. Acts xx. 22.

towards that nation who once took me captive and made havoc of the menservants and maidservants of my father's house? I was freeborn according to the flesh; I am born of a father who was a decurion; but I sold my noble rank —I blush not to state it, nor am I sorry—for the profit of others; in short, I am a slave in Christ to a foreign nation for the unspeakable glory of the *eternal life which is in Christ Jesus our Lord.*

11. And if my own know me not, *a prophet hath no honour in his own country.* Perchance we are not of *the one fold,* nor have *one God and Father.* As he saith, *He that is not with me is against me, and he that gathereth not with me scattereth abroad.* It is not meet that *one pulleth down and another buildeth up. I seek not mine own.*

It was not any grace in me, but God that *put this earnest care into my heart,* that I should be one of the *hunters or fishers* whom long ago God foreshowed would come *in the last days.*

12. Men look askance at me. What shall I do, O Lord? I am exceedingly despised. Lo, around me are thy sheep torn to pieces and spoiled, and that too by the robbers aforesaid, by the orders of Coroticus with hostile disposition.

Far from the love of God is he who betrays Christians into the hands of the Scots and Picts. *Ravening wolves* have swallowed up the flock of the Lord which verily. in Ireland was growing up excellently with the greatest care. And the sons and daughters of Scottic chieftains who were monks and virgins of Christ I cannot reckon. Wherefore, *be not pleased with the wrong done to the just; even unto hell it shall not please thee.*

10, Rom. vi. 23.
11. John iv. 44; John x. 16; Eph. iv. 6; Mal. ii. 10; Matt. xii. 30; Ecclus. xxxiv. 28; 1 Cor. xiii. 5; 2 Cor. viii. 16; Jer. xvi. 16; Acts ii. 17.   12. Acts xx. 29; Ecclus. ix. 17.

13. Which of the saints would not shudder to jest or feast with such men ? They have filled their houses with the spoil of dead Christians. They live by plunder. Wretched men, they know not that it is poison; they offer the deadly food to their friends and sons; just as Eve did not understand that verily it was death that she handed to her husband. So are all they who do wrong ; they work death as their eternal punishment.

14. This is the custom of the Roman Gauls :—They send holy and fit men to the Franks and other heathen with many thousands of solidi to redeem baptized captives. Thou rather slayest and sellest them to a foreign *nation which knows not God.* Thou handest over *the members of Christ* as it were to a brothel. What manner of hope in God hast thou, or has he who consents with thee, or who holds converse with thee in words of flattery ? God will judge ; for it is written, *Not only those who commit evil, but those that consent with them shall be damned.*

15. I know not *what I should say, or what I should speak* further about the departed ones of the sons of God, whom the sword has touched harshly above measure. For it is written, *Weep with them that weep,* and again, *If one member suffer, let all the members suffer with it.* On this account the Church bewails and laments her sons and daughters whom the sword has not as yet slain, but who are banished and carried off to distant lands where sin openly, grievously, and shamelessly abounds. There freemen are put up for sale, Christians are reduced to slavery, and, worst of all, to most degraded, most vile, and apostate Picts.

16. Therefore in sadness and grief shall I cry aloud : O most lovely and beloved brethren, and sons whom *I*

14. 1 Thess. iv. 5 ; 1 Cor. vi. 15 ; Rom. i. 32.
15 John xii. 49 ; Rom. xii. 15 ; 1 Cor. xii. 26.

begot in Christ—I cannot reckon them—what shall I do for
you ? ¯ I am not worthy to come to the aid of either God
or men. *The wickedness of the wicked hath prevailed against
us. We are become* as it were *strangers.* Perchance they
do not believe that we receive *one baptism,* and that we
have *one God and Father.* It is in their eyes a disgraceful
thing that we were born in Ireland. As he saith, *Have ye
not one God ? Why do ye, each one, forsake his neighbour ?*

17. Therefore, I grieve for you, I grieve, O ye most
dear to me. But again, I rejoice within myself. *I have
not laboured* for nought, and my going abroad was not *in
vain.* And there happened a crime so horrid and unspeakable ! Thanks be to God, it was as baptized believers
that ye departed from the world to Paradise. I can see
you. Ye have begun to remove to where *there shall be no
night nor sorrow nor death any more ;* but *ye shall leap like
calves loosened from their bands, and ye shall tread down the
wicked, and they shall be ashes under your feet.*

18. Ye therefore shall reign with apostles and prophets
and martyrs. Ye shall take everlasting kingdoms, as he
himself witnesseth, saying, *They shall come from the east and
west, and shall sit down with Abraham and Isaac and Jacob in
the kingdom of heaven. Without are dogs and sorcerers and
murderers ;* and *liars and false swearers shall have their part in
the lake of everlasting fire.* Not without just cause the
apostle saith, *Where the righteous shall scarcely be saved,
where shall the sinner and the ungodly transgressor of the law
recognize himself ?*

19. Wherefore then, where shall Coroticus with his
accursed followers, rebels against Christ, where shall they
see themselves ?—they who distribute baptized damsels as
rewards, and that for the sake of a wretched temporal

16. 1 Cor. iv. 15 ; Ps. lxv. 3 ; Ps. lxix. 8 ; Eph. iv. 5 ; Mal. ii. 10.
17. Phil. ii. 16 ; Rev. xxii. 5 ; xxi. 4 ; Mal. iv. 2.
18. Matt. vii. 11 ; Rev. xxii. 15 ; xxi. 8 ; 1 Pet. iv. 18.

kingdom, which verily passes away in a moment like a cloud or *smoke which is* verily *dispersed by the wind. So shall the* deceitful *wicked perish at the presence of the Lord; but let the righteous feast* in great constancy with Christ. *They shall judge nations, and rule* over ungodly kings for ever and ever. Amen.

20. *I testify before God and his angels* that it will be so as he has signified to my unskilfulness. The words are not mine, but of God and the apostles and prophets, who have never lied, which I have set forth in Latin. *He that believeth shall be saved, but he that believeth not shall be damned.* God hath spoken.

21. I beseech very much that whatever servant of God be ready, he be the bearer of this letter, that on no account it be suppressed or concealed by anyone, but much rather be read in the presence of all the people, yea, in the presence of Coroticus himself; if so be that God may inspire them to amend their lives to God some time; so that even though late they may repent of their impious doings—murderer of the brethren of the Lord!—and may liberate the baptized women captives whom they had taken, so that they may deserve to live to God, and be made whole, both here and in eternity.

Peace—to the Father, and to the Son, and to the Holy Ghost. Amen.

---

19. Wisd. v. 15 ; Ps lxviii. 2, 3 ; Wisd. iii. 8.
20. 1 Tim. v. 21 ; Mark xvi. 16.

BILLING AND SONS, LTD., PRINTERS, GUILDFORD, ENGLAND

Printed in the USA
CPSIA information can be obtained
at www.ICGtesting.com
CBHW061709120624
9946CB00040B/265